✳ Smithsonian

SPACE DISCOVERIES

by TAMRA B. ORR

CAPSTONE PRESS
a capstone imprint

Smithsonian is published by Capstone Press
1710 Roe Crest Drive North Mankato, Minnesota 56003
www.mycapstone.com

Copyright © 2019 Capstone Press All rights reserved. No part of this publication may be reproduced in whole or in part, or stored in a retrieval system, or transmitted in any form or by any means, electronic, mechanical, photocopying, recording, or otherwise, without written permission of the publisher.
The name of the Smithsonian Institution and the sunburst logo are registered trademarks of the Smithsonian Institution. For more information, please visit www.si.edu.

Library of Congress Cataloging-in-Publication Data
Names: Orr, Tamra, author.
Title: Space discoveries / by Tamra B. Orr.
Description: North Mankato, Minnesota : Capstone Press, [2019] | Series: Smithsonian. Marvelous discoveries | Audience: Age 7–10. Identifiers: LCCN 2018010992 (print) | LCCN 2018014707 (ebook) | ISBN 9781543526240 (eBook PDF) | ISBN 9781543526165 (hardcover) | ISBN 9781543526202 (pbk.) Subjects: LCSH: Outer space—Juvenile literature. | Outer space—Exploration—Juvenile literature. Classification: LCC QB500.22 (ebook) | LCC QB500.22 .O77 2019 (print) | DDC 520—dc23 LC record available at https://lccn.loc.gov/2018010992

Editorial Credits
Michelle Hasselius, editor; Heidi Thompson, designer; Svetlana Zhurkin, media researcher; Kris Wilfahrt, production specialist

Our very special thanks to Valerie Neal, Chair, Space History Department at the National Air and Space Museum for her review. Capstone would also like to thank the following at Smithsonian Enterprises: Kealy Gordon, Product Development Manager; Ellen Nanney, Licensing Manager; Brigid Ferraro, Vice President, Education and Consumer Products; and Carol LeBlanc, Senior Vice President, Education and Consumer Products.

Photo Credits
AP Images: Neal Hamberg, 28 (left); B. Saxton/NRAO/AUI/NSF, 28 (right); ESO: L. Calçada/M. Kornmesser, 21 (back); NASA: 12, 17 (inset), 19, 23, 27, Ames/JPL-Caltech, 24-25, Ames/JPL-Caltech/T. Pyle, 26, Charles Babir, 16 (right), Chris Gunn, 13, Dana Berry/Sky Works Digital, 21 (inset), ESA/A. Feild (STScI), 9, ESA/H. Bond (STScI)/M. Barstow (University of Leicester), 29, Goddard Space Flight Center/CI Lab, 20, Goddard/Arizona State University, 22 (top), JPL, cover (bottom), 10, JPL/Space Science Institute, 4, JPL/USGS, 8, JPL-Caltech, 6, 11, Ken Ulbrich, 18, SDO, 17 (back); Newscom: Zuma Press/Mainichi Newspaper, 15; Shutterstock: Guilherme Mesquita, 5, Kathy Hutchins, 16 (left), Radoslaw Lecyk, 22 (bottom), Rosamund Parkinson, 7, seecreateimages, cover (background), Vadim Sadovski, 14

Quote Sources
Page 7, "Small Asteroid Is Earth's Constant Companion." 15 June 2016. NASA. https://www.nasa.gov/feature/jpl/small-asteroid-is-earths-constant-companion

Page 13, "Hubble Reveals Observable Universe Contains 10 Times More Galaxies Than Previously Thought." 13 October 2016. NASA. https://www.nasa.gov/feature/goddard/2016/hubble-reveals-observable-universe-contains-10-times-more-galaxies-than-previously-thought

Printed and bound in the United States
PA017

TABLE OF CONTENTS

ENDLESS EXPLORATION

Have you ever looked up at the night sky and wondered what is out there? What hasn't been discovered yet—new planets, more galaxies, little green men?

Since the first telescope was invented more than 400 years ago, people have been looking up to the sky. The drive to find out what is out there has grown since then. In the 1960s, the United States began sending spaceships and astronauts to the moon. Since then space missions and space probes have discovered moons, planets, and stars that we didn't know existed before. What else is still up there waiting to be discovered?

MORE MOONS

EARTH'S MINI MOON?

The Earth is being followed—by a mini moon. In 2016 NASA scientists spotted a large asteroid circling Earth. The asteroid was named 2016 H03. It is 120 to 300 feet (36.6 to 91.4 meters) wide. Nicknamed the mini moon, the asteroid moves around our planet like a satellite. Both the asteroid and Earth orbit the sun together.

The 2016 H03 asteroid is also called a near-Earth companion.

Sun ▶·

Earth ▶·

◀2016 HO3

"Since 2016 H03 loops around our planet, but never ventures very far away as we both go around the sun, we refer to it as a quasi-satellite of Earth."

—Paul Chodas, manager of the Planetary Defense Coordination Office in Hawaii

Haleakala Observatory in Hawaii, where the asteroid was first spotted

The newly discovered asteroid might be NASA's next space mission. Scientists believe a space probe could reach the asteroid in about 65 days.

A MOON FOR NEPTUNE

In 2013 scientists discovered that the planet Neptune has another moon. The new moon is called S/2004 N1. It's 12.5 miles (20.1 kilometers) wide. Scientist Mark Showalter was looking through a pile of photographs taken by the Hubble Space Telescope. The Hubble uses a digital camera to take detailed photos of the universe. Showalter saw an unexpected dot in these photos. That dot turned out to be S/2004 N1. Scientists plan to give S/2004 N1 a new name in the future. For now, most experts refer to it as "that little moon."

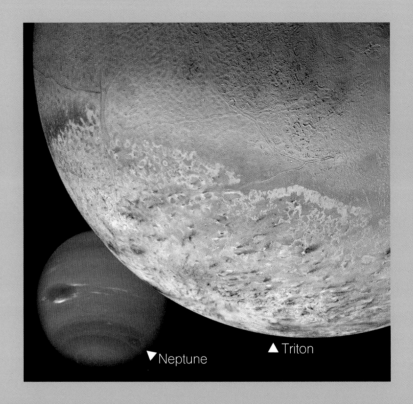

▼Neptune   ▲ Triton

Triton is Neptune's largest moon. It's 1,680 miles (2,704 km) wide.

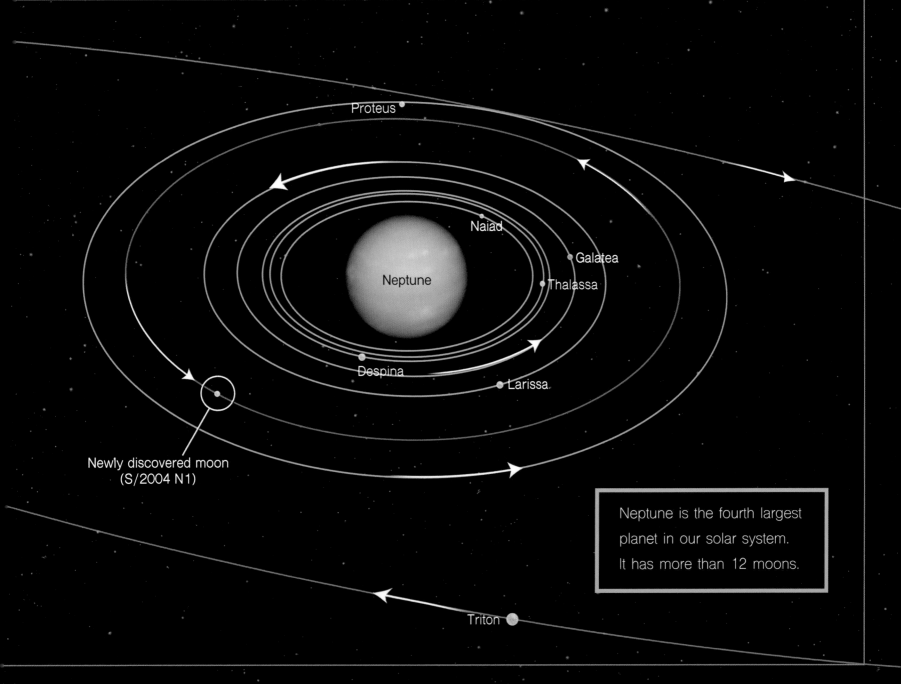

Proteus

Naiad

Galatea

Neptune

Thalassa

Despina

Larissa

Newly discovered moon
(S/2004 N1)

Neptune is the fourth largest
planet in our solar system.
It has more than 12 moons.

Triton

JUPITER AND JUNO

On August 5, 2011, the *Juno* space probe was launched to study the planet Jupiter. The unmanned spacecraft entered Jupiter's orbit on July 4, 2016. Since then *Juno* has circled the planet multiple times. It's recorded new information about Jupiter's size, temperature, and weather. The space probe has also taken stunning pictures. Scientists were surprised by Jupiter's bright colors. *Juno* will remain in space until at least July 2018.

The *Juno* space probe cost more than $1 billion to build. It travels 164,700 miles (265,059 km) per hour.

Juno is not the first space probe to study Jupiter. NASA's *Pioneer* and *Voyager* probes flew by the planet in the 1970s. They took basic pictures and measurements of Jupiter.

◄ Juno

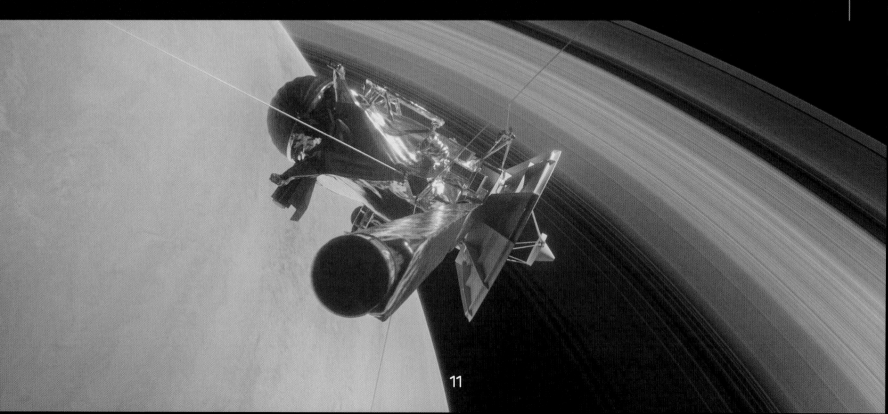

CASSINI'S DISCOVERIES

In 1997 NASA launched the *Cassini* space probe to study Saturn.

launched	1997
first mission completed	June 2008 (mission extended to September 2010)
traveled	4.9 billion miles (7.8 billion km)
collected	635 gigabytes of data
captured	more than 453,000 photographs
discovered	6 moons, 3 seas, and 2 oceans
orbited Saturn	294 times

GALAXIES FAR AWAY

In 2016 astronomers were shocked to discover that the universe is much bigger than they thought. At first, scientists thought there were 200 billion galaxies in space. Now astronomers believe the universe has 2 trillion galaxies!

This discovery is based on photographs from the Hubble Space Telescope. Astronomers were able to create a 3D map of the universe based on this new data.

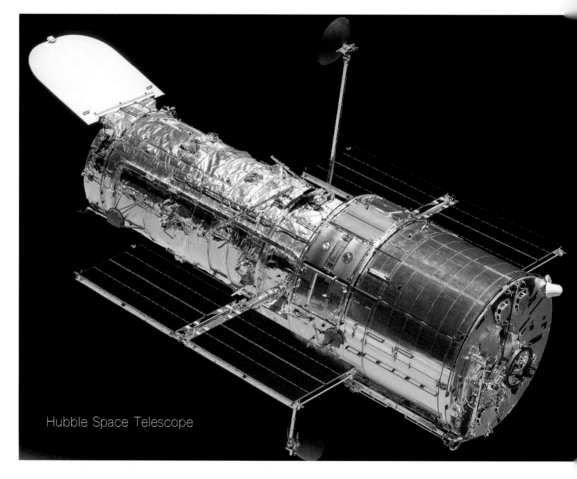

Hubble Space Telescope

"It boggles the mind that over 90 percent of the galaxies in the universe have yet to be studied. Who knows what interesting properties we will find when we observe these galaxies with the next generation of telescopes?"
—Christopher Conselice, astrophysicist

The new James Webb Space Telescope will be able to look farther into space than any other telescope ever used.

WET, RED PLANET

Today the planet Mars is frozen and dry. But NASA researchers have discovered that may have not always been the case. In 2017 researchers discovered that a massive asteroid crashed into Mars about 3 billion years ago. It landed right in one of the planet's largest oceans. The asteroid created mega tsunamis all over Mars. The push and pull of water from the tsunamis left a large crater on the planet's surface. Scientists believe this crater will prove that Mars once had lakes, rivers, seas, and oceans—just like Earth. That means it might have had life on it too.

Researchers believe that the tsunami waves on Mars were almost 500 feet (152 m) tall. In 2011 the tsunami waves that crashed into Japan were 128 feet (39 m) tall. The 2005 tsunami in Indonesia had waves 100 feet (30.5 m) high.

the 2011 tsunami in Miyagi, Japan

THE SPACE TRAVEL BUSINESS

Launching a rocket into space is exciting—and expensive. And rockets can only be used once. But this is changing. Private companies, such as SpaceX, have found ways to build recyclable rockets. These rockets were designed to return to Earth and be used again. So far SpaceX has sent these rockets to the International Space Station (ISS) and back. Currently the company is trying to send a crew of astronauts into space. To do this they will use their *Dragon* spacecraft, a rocket that can fit up to seven people inside. The company hopes to send humans to Mars one day.

Elon Musk founded SpaceX. In the *Iron Man* movies, Robert Downey Jr. based his portrayal of Tony Stark on Musk.

SPACEX'S DSCOVR SATELLITE

In 2015 SpaceX partnered with the U.S. Air Force and NASA to launch a satellite into deep space. The DSCOVR satellite was built to keep a close eye on the sun's solar flares. Solar flares are sudden bursts of radiation from the sun's surface. These flares can effect radios, power lines, and cell phones on Earth. The DSCOVR satellite sends a warning to scientists around the world if a flare is detected.

In Titusville, Florida, scientists get the DSCOVR satellite ready to launch.

SpaceX is not the only private company in the space travel business. A number of other companies are lining up for the chance to launch rockets into space. Large companies like Boeing and Lockheed Martin usually build military planes and passenger airlines. Now they are building spacecraft to take astronauts and needed equipment to the ISS.

The Sierra Nevada Corporation has created a mini space shuttle called the Dream Chaser. The Dream Chaser can carry two to seven people. It is scheduled to start sending supplies to the ISS around 2020.

Lockheed Martin's *Orion* ground test vehicle arrived at the Kennedy Space Center on April 21, 2012.

GOLDEN SKIES

On August 17, 2017, there was a huge explosion—complete with fireworks. Two stars crashed into each other, filling the universe with gold, silver, and platinum. The event is known as a kilonova. You couldn't see it in the sky, but astronomers were watching. Back on Earth, satellite and telescope sensors went off across the world. For the first time in history, scientists had the technology to know where to look to see this rare event.

Astronomers call the dust and debris from the crash "neutron star guts."

Experts believe the two stars were swirling around each other at one thousand times per second before they crashed into each other.

HOME, SWEET LAVA TUBE

In October 2017 researchers from Japan spotted a giant hole in the moon. The hole leads down to a long, hollow lava tube. The tube is huge. Scientists believe it could hold a city as big as Philadelphia inside.

The Earth also has lava tubes. But none of them are close to the size as the one found on the moon.

Thurston lava tube in Hawaii

A lava tube is formed when lava flows under the ground. The outside of the tube crusts over. Astronauts could use lava tubes to protect themselves from meteor storms and extreme temperatures on the moon. Perhaps one day, these tubes could even be used to create the first human civilization on the moon. People could live on the moon for weeks or longer.

Astronauts cannot survive for more than three days on the moon. Their spacesuits are not designed to be on the moon for long periods of time.

Astronaut Eugene A. Cernan drove the Lunar Roving Vehicle on the moon in December 1972.

KEPLER 10C

Look at that! It's Godzilla! No, we're not talking about the fictional movie sea monster. Godzilla is a giant planet. Using the Kepler Space Telescope, astronomers discovered the planet in May 2011. It's called Kepler 10c. It's 560 light-years away from Earth. The planet is 17 times heavier than Earth and twice the size. Scientists believe it is 11 billion years old.

Scientists also call the planet mega-Earth.

Kepler 10c

Kepler 10c takes 45 days to circle around its sunlike star. Earth takes 365 days to circle around our sun.

KEPLER 37B

Finding the planet Kepler 37b was a challenge for scientists. It is only about one-third the size of Earth. That's even smaller than Mercury, the smallest planet in our solar system. NASA scientists found the planet in February 2013. It's located about 210 light-years away from Earth.

Kepler 37b may be little, but it is hot. Scientists believe that the planet's average temperature is about 800 degrees Fahrenheit (426 degrees Celsius). That is hot enough to melt the zinc inside of a penny!

THE KEPLER SPACE TELESCOPE

One of the reasons that the world knows so much about space is because of space telescopes, such as the Hubble Space Telescope and the Kepler Space Telescope. These telescopes are like floating science labs, equipped with recorders, cameras, and computer chips. All of the information they gather is sent back to Earth for scientists to study.

The Kepler Space Telescope was launched into space in 2009. It has 42 cameras. The telescope is pointed at a single spot in the sky. Built-in sensors watch the spot carefully. The Kepler Space Telescope has found more than 4,000 planets so far.

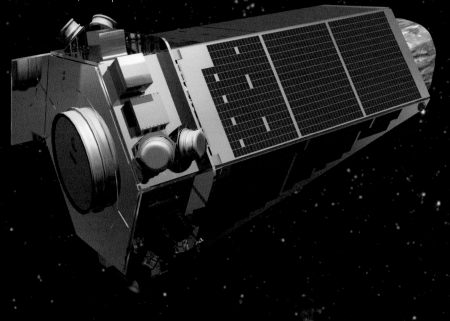

THE DIAMOND STAR

Imagine a diamond the size of Earth. It would have trillions of trillions of carats. Astronomers spotted a diamond this size in 2014. Named PSR J2222-0137, the diamond is about 11 billion years old. It's 900 light-years away from Earth.

The largest diamond on Earth is the Golden Jubilee. It has 546 carats. The softball–sized diamond was found in South Africa.

A white dwarf star and PSR J2222-0137 orbit around each other.

This diamond is formed from a white dwarf star. After a star ages and dies, it turns into a white dwarf star. Over billions of years, the dwarf star crystallizes. It gets smaller, colder, and dimmer. The inside of the white dwarf star turns into a diamond.

white dwarf star called Sirius B

Scientists believe that our sun will become a white dwarf star in 5 billion years. About 2 billion years after that, it will crystallize. Then the sun will become a giant diamond in the center of our solar system.

GLOSSARY

asteroid (AS-tuh-royd)—a large rock that travels through space

astronaut (AS-truh-nawt)—a person who is trained to live and work in space

astronomer (uh-STAH-nuh-muhr)—a scientist who studies stars, planets, and other objects in space

carat (KAR-uht)—a unit for measuring the weight of precious gems and metals

crater (KRAY-tuhr)—a hole made when large pieces of rock crash into a planet's or moon's surface

crystallize (KRISS-tuh-lize)—to form crystals

galaxy (GAL-uhk-see)—a large group of stars and planets

gigabyte (GIH-guh-byte)—a unit used to measure the amount of data storage; a gigabyte is 1 billion bytes

light-year (LITE-yihr)—a unit for measuring the distance in space

meteor (MEE-tee-ur)—a chunk of metal or stone that falls from space; a meteor is also called a shooting star

NASA (NASS-uh)—a U.S. government agency that does research on flight and space exploration

orbit (OR-bit)—the path an object follows as it goes around a sun or a planet

platinum (PLAT-n-uhm)—a valuable silver-white metal that is often used in jewelry

satellite (SAT-uh-lite)—an object used for communicating or collecting information that moves around Earth in space

solar system (SOH-lur SISS-tuhm)—a sun and all the planets, moons, and smaller objects moving around it

space probe (SPAYSS PROHB)—a spacecraft without a crew that is used to explore space

tsunami (tsoo-NAH-mee)—a very large wave

CRITICAL THINKING QUESTIONS

1. Describe what happens during a kilonova.

2. Using the Kepler Space Telescope, scientists have discovered the planets Kepler 10c and Kepler 37b. Name other planet that scientists have found with this telescope. What makes this planet unique?

3. In your own words, describe how a diamond is formed in space.

READ MORE

O'Hearn, Michael. *Awesome Space Robots*. Robots. Mankato, Minn.: Capstone Press, 2013.

Simon, Seymour. *Exoplanets*. New York: HarperCollins, 2018.

Vogt, Gregory L. *Building Reusable Rockets*. Destination Space. Lake Elmo, Minn.: Focus Readers, 2018.

INTERNET SITES

Use FactHound to find Internet sites related to this book.

Visit *www.facthound.com*

Just type in 9781543526165 and go.

Check out projects, games and lots more at
www.capstonekids.com

INDEX